Colombian Girls

Hot Sexy Colombian Lingerie Girls Models Pictures

By **PHOTO ART LOVER**

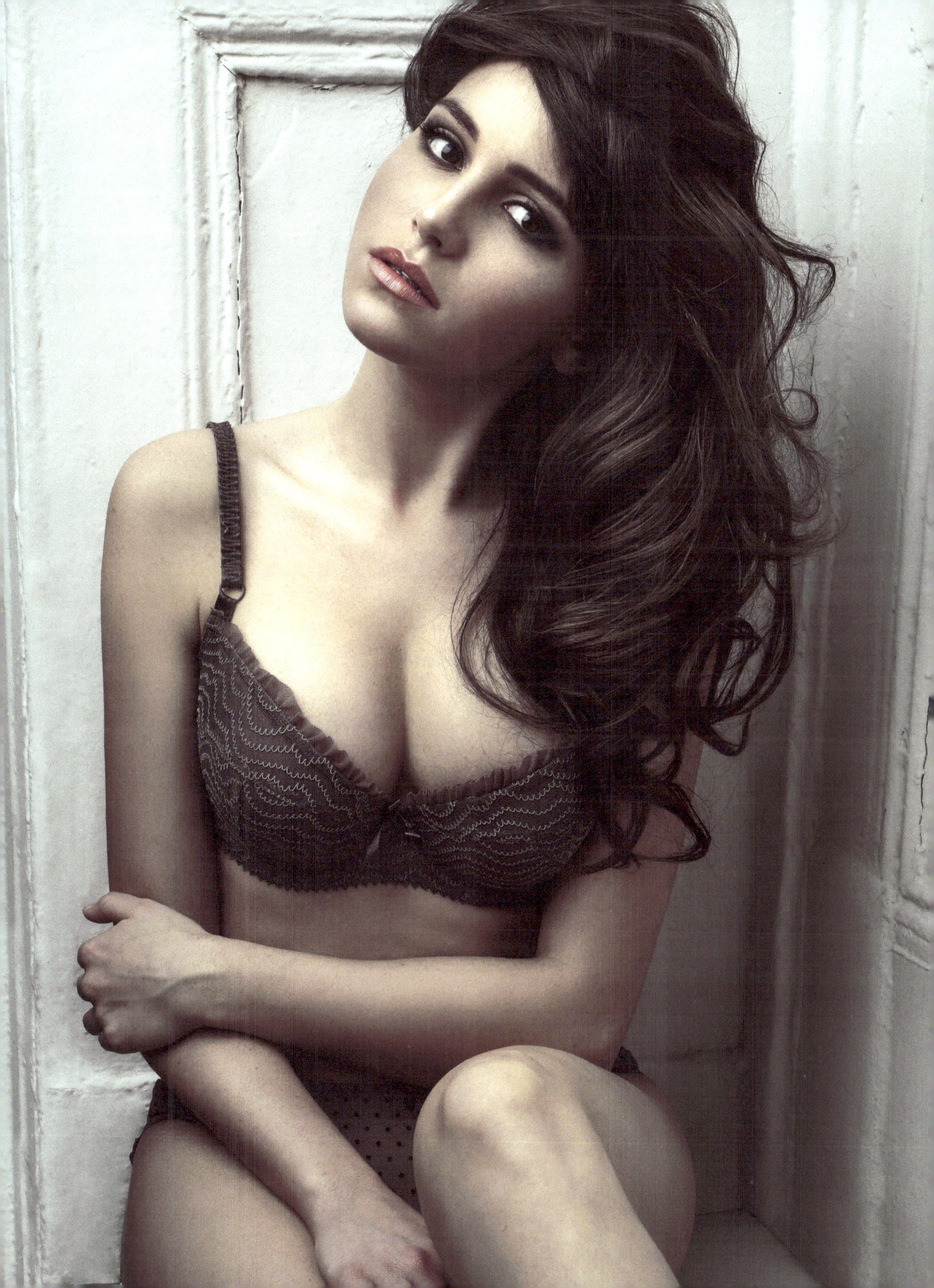

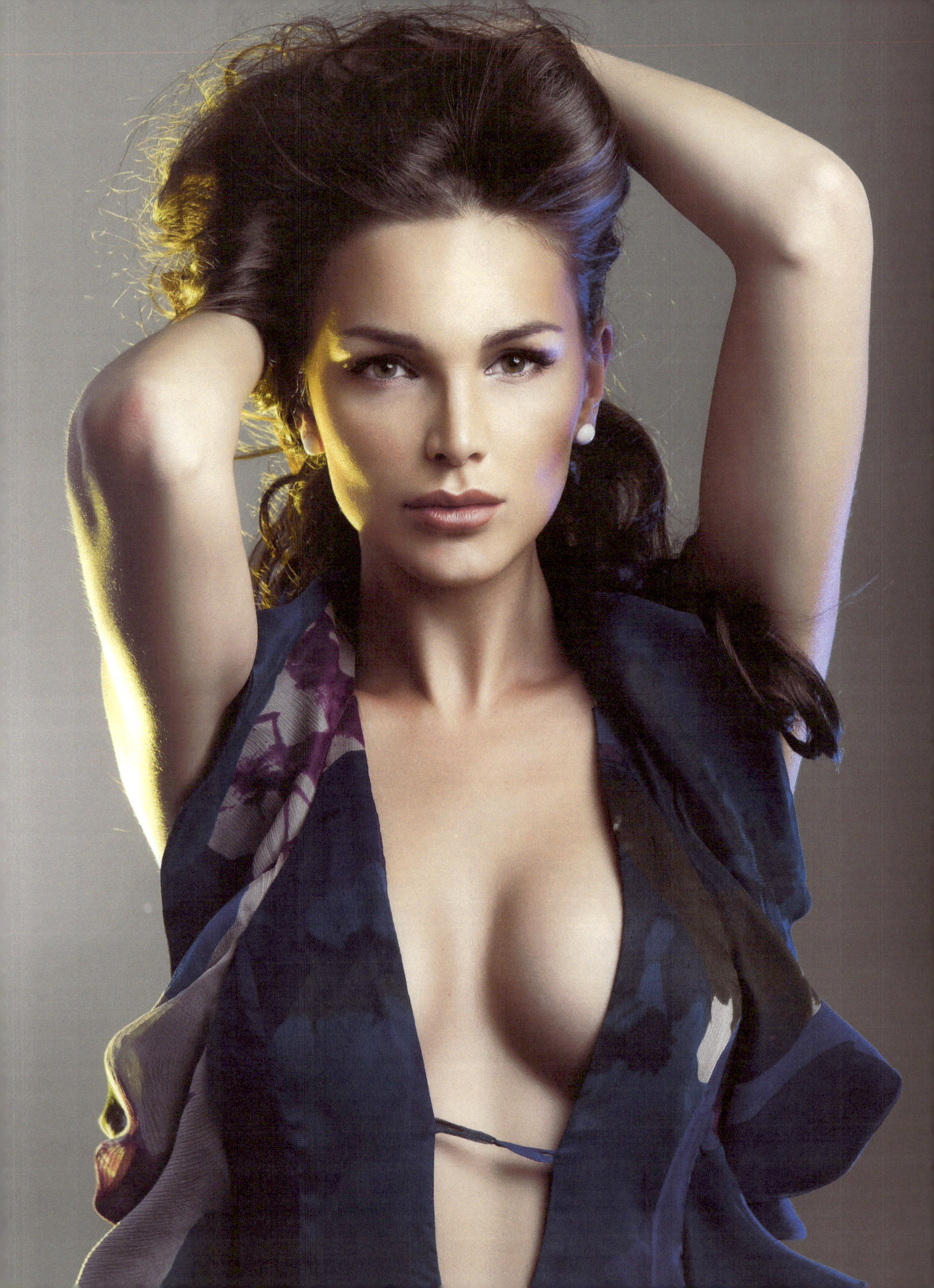

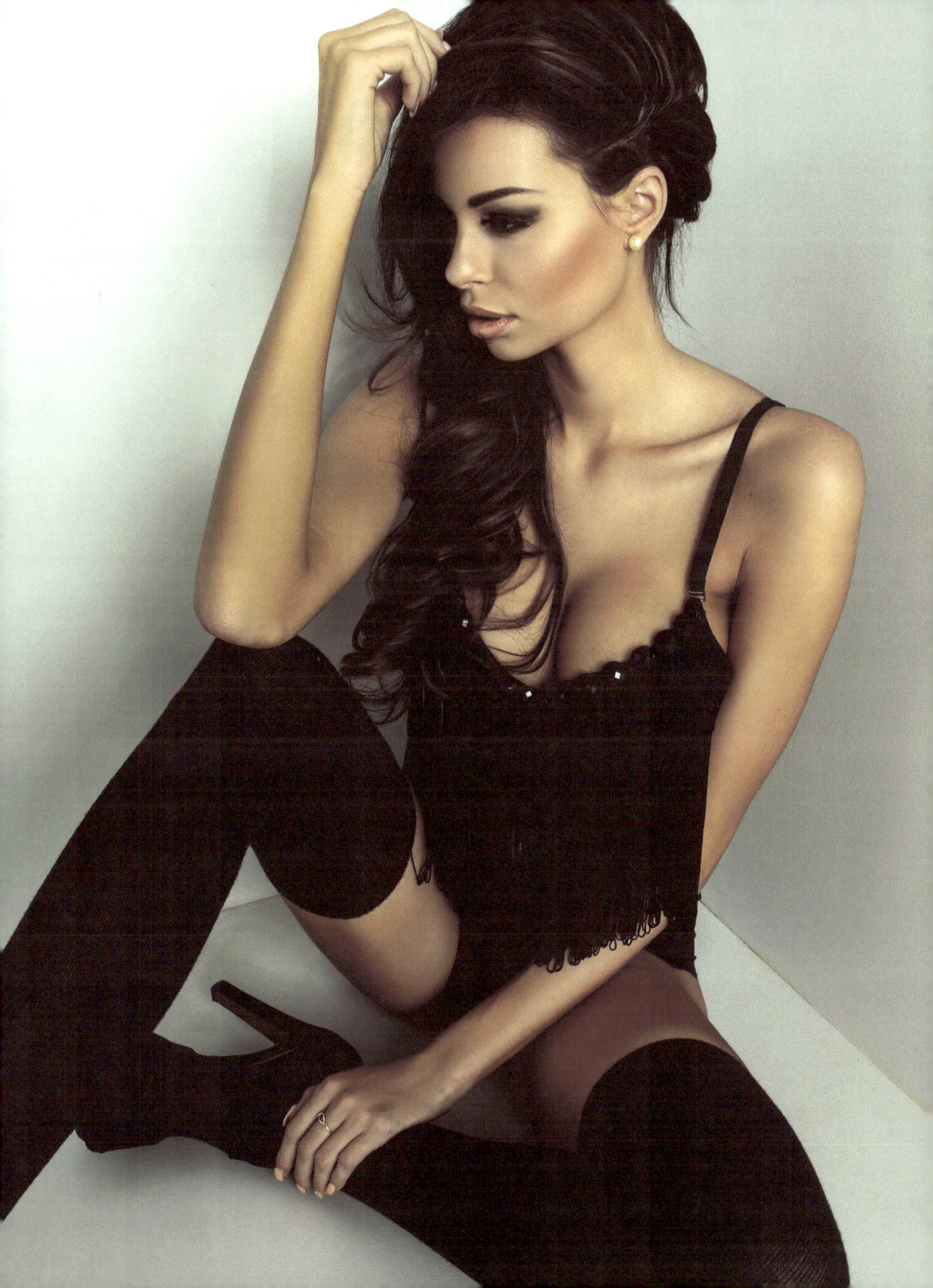

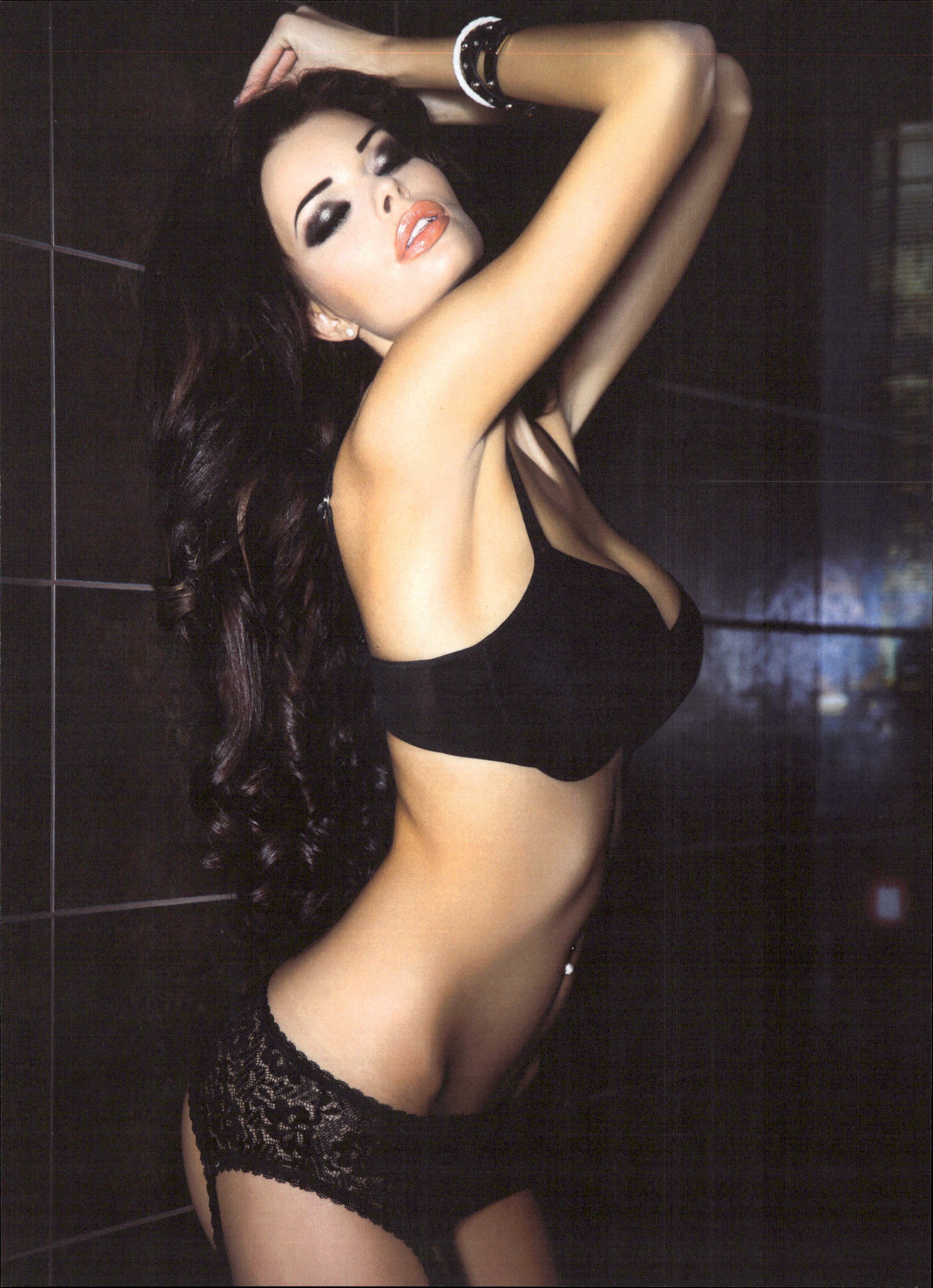

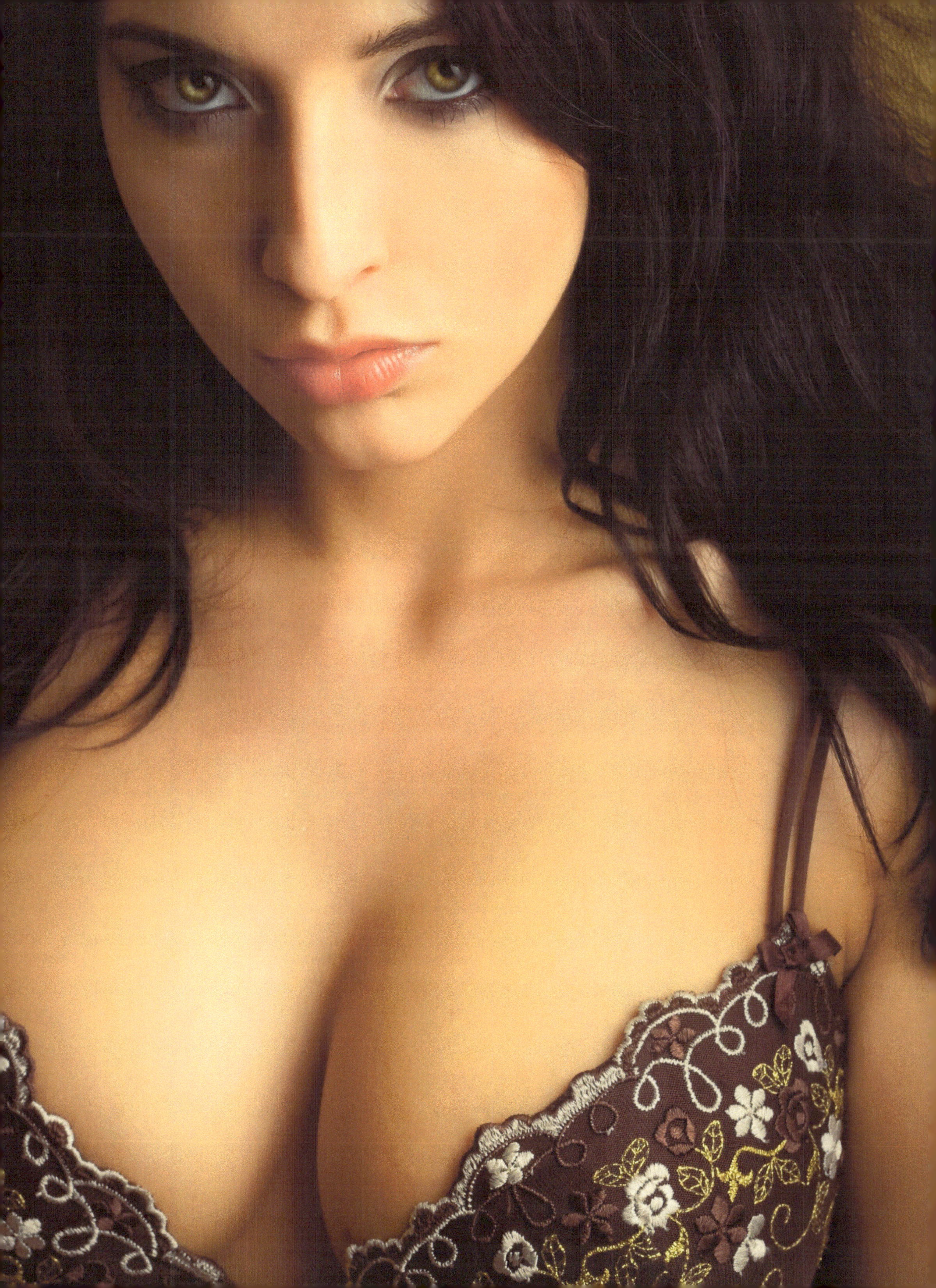

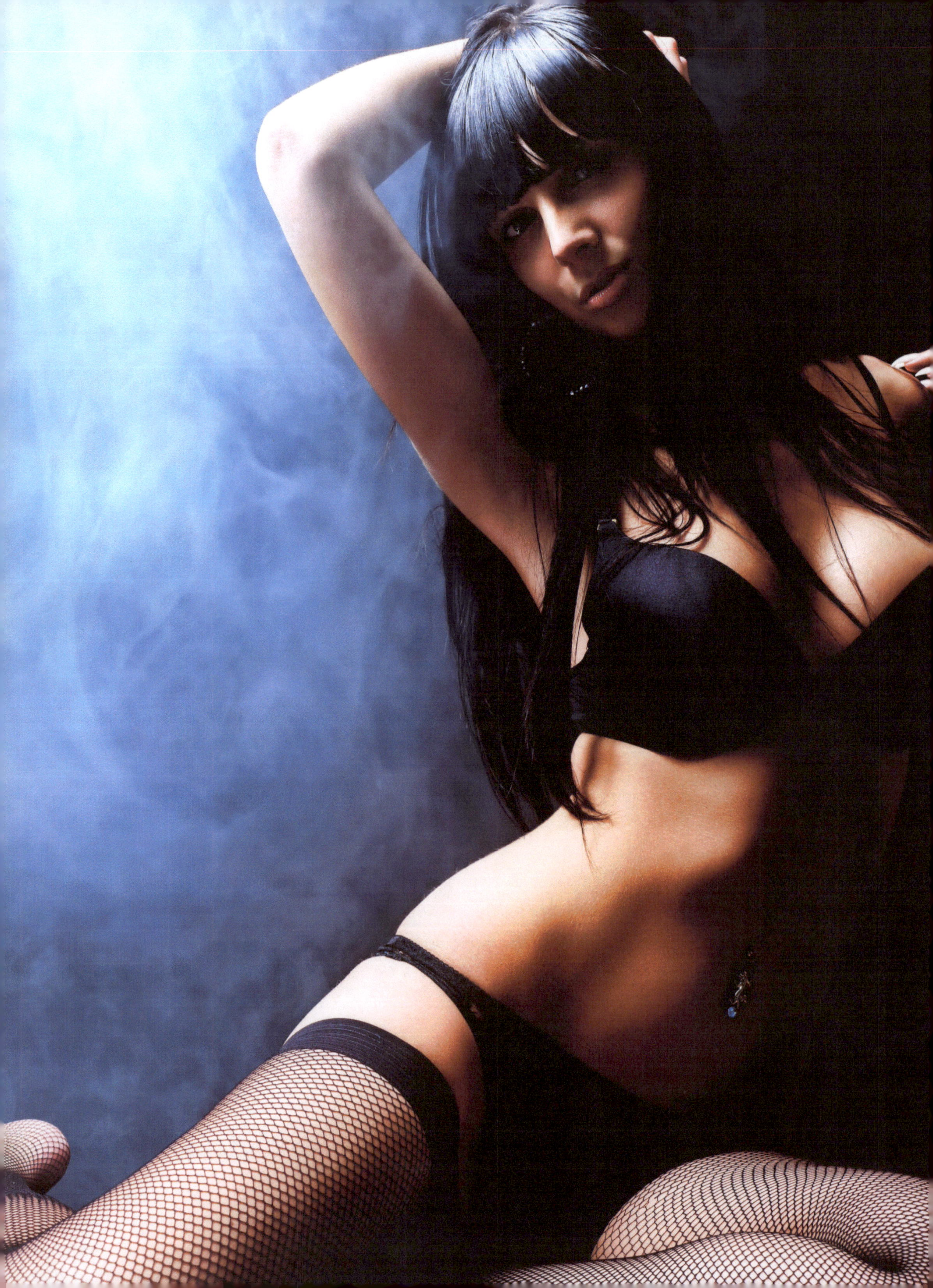

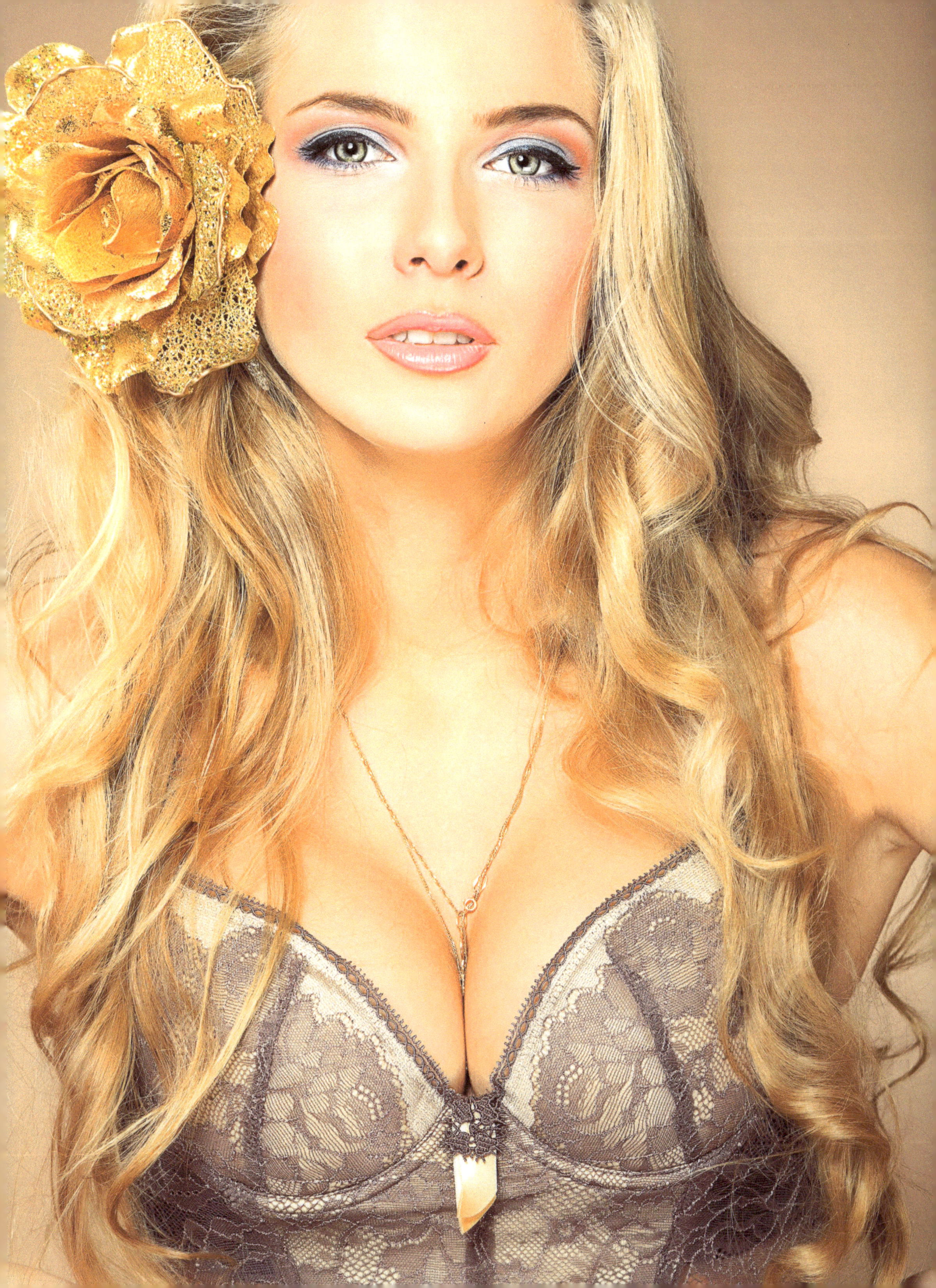

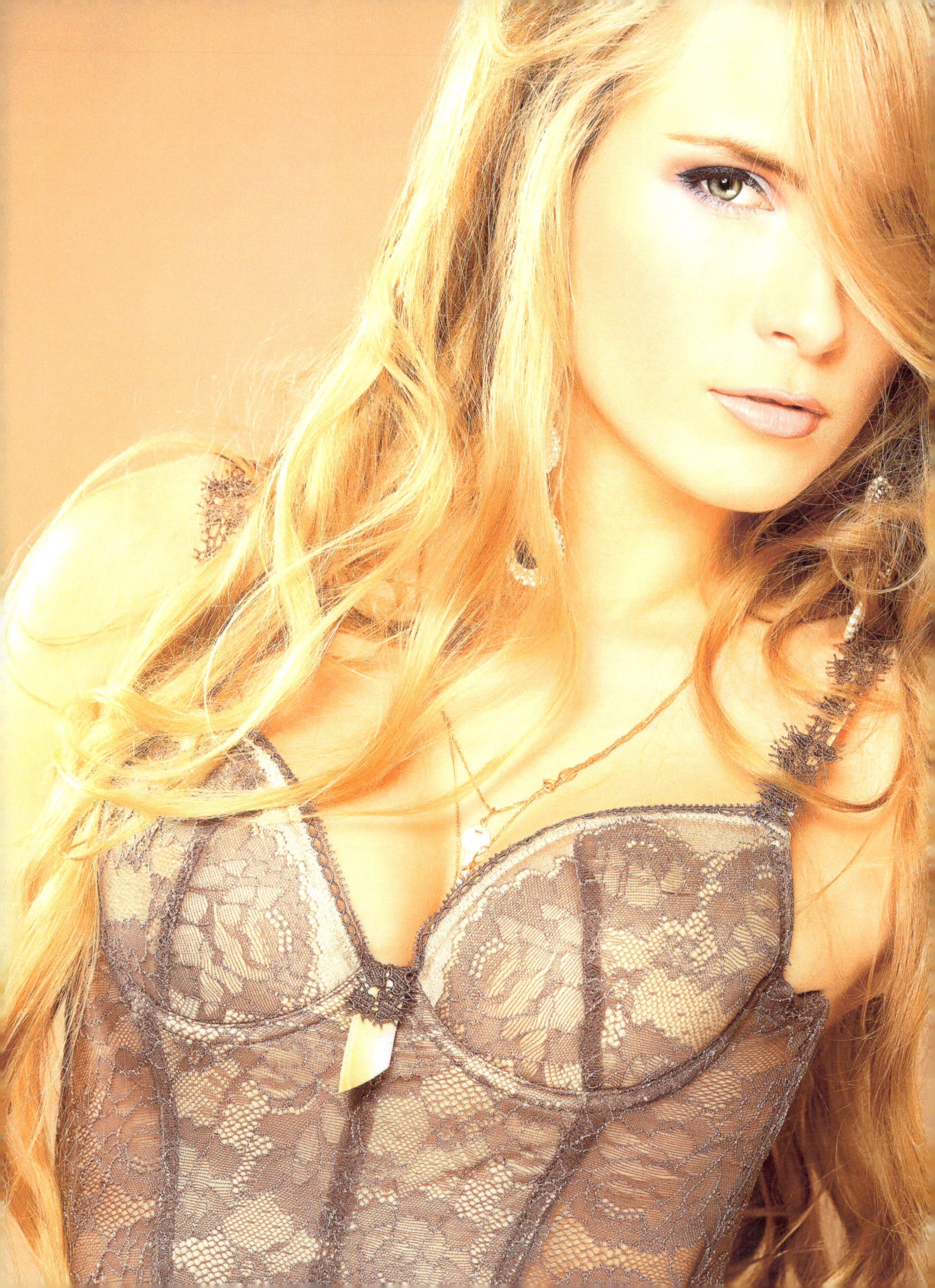

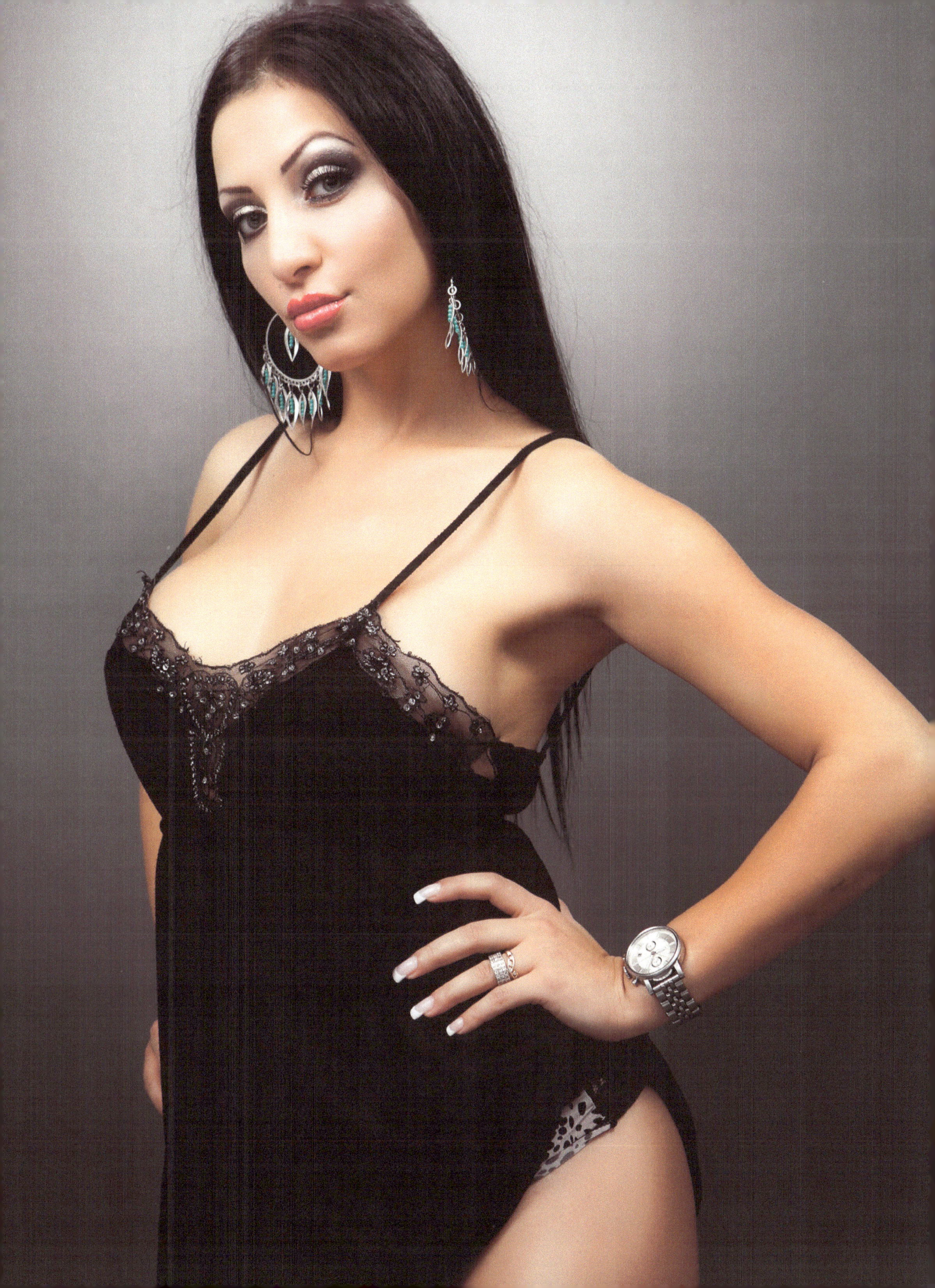

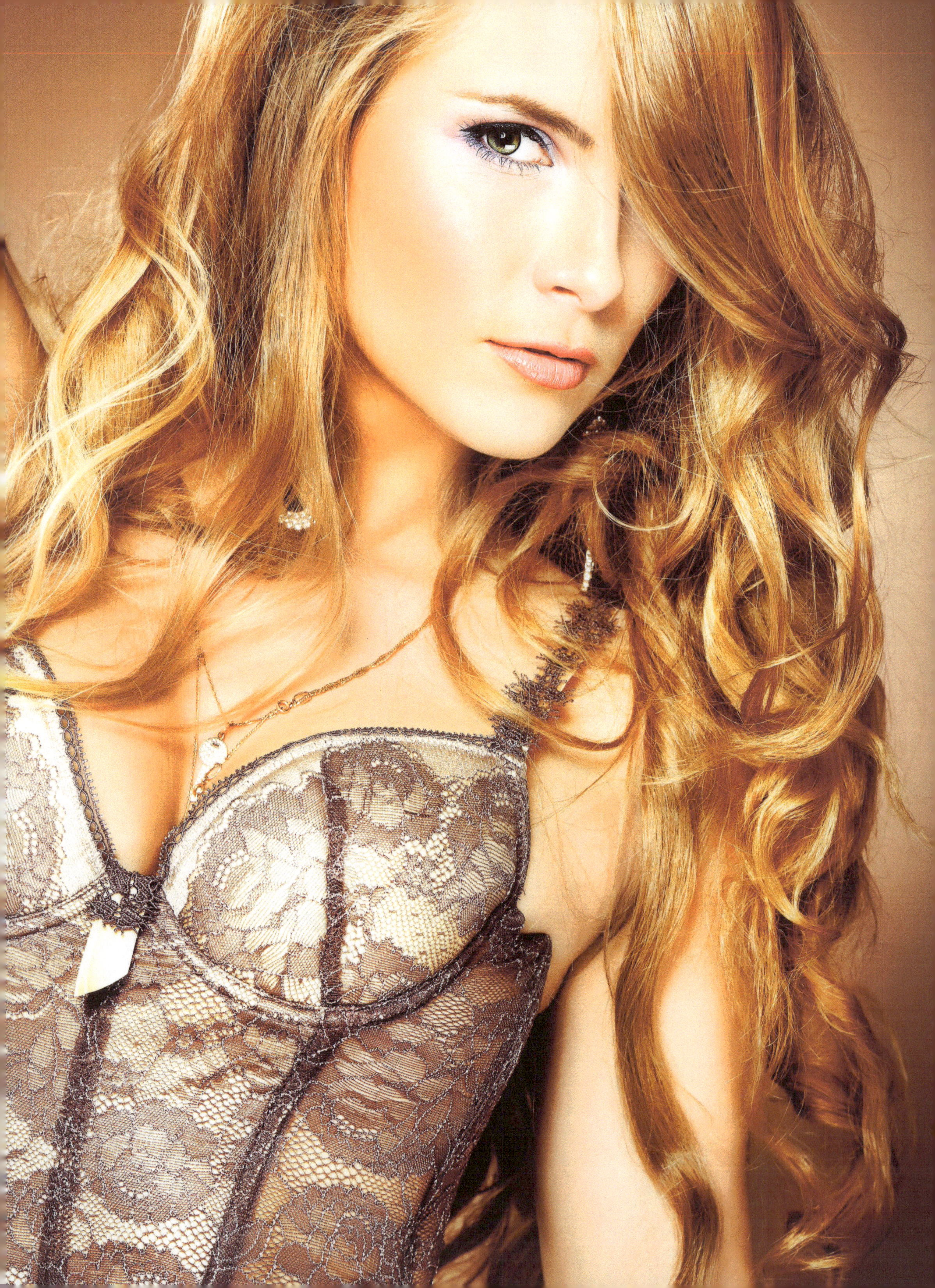

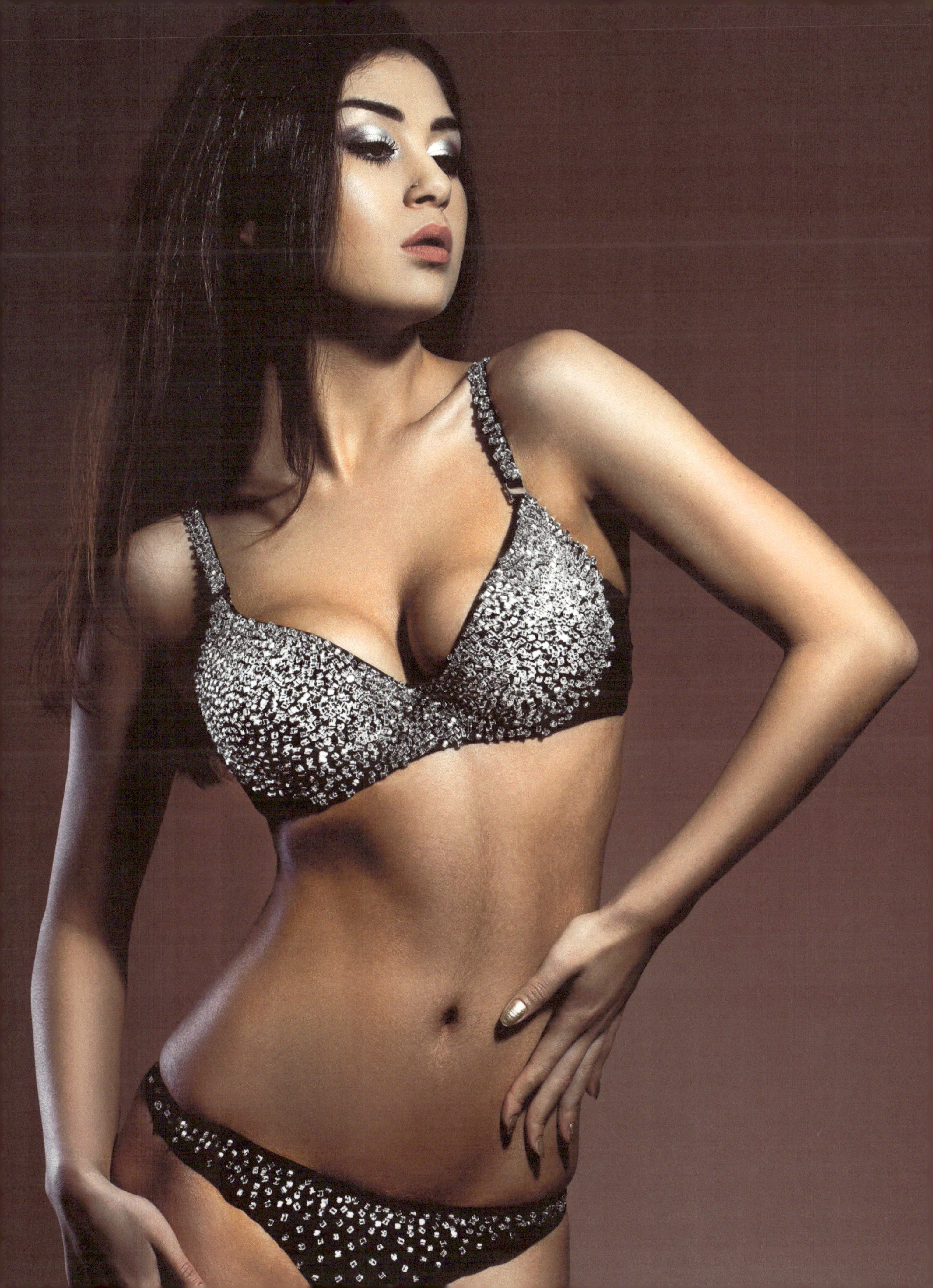

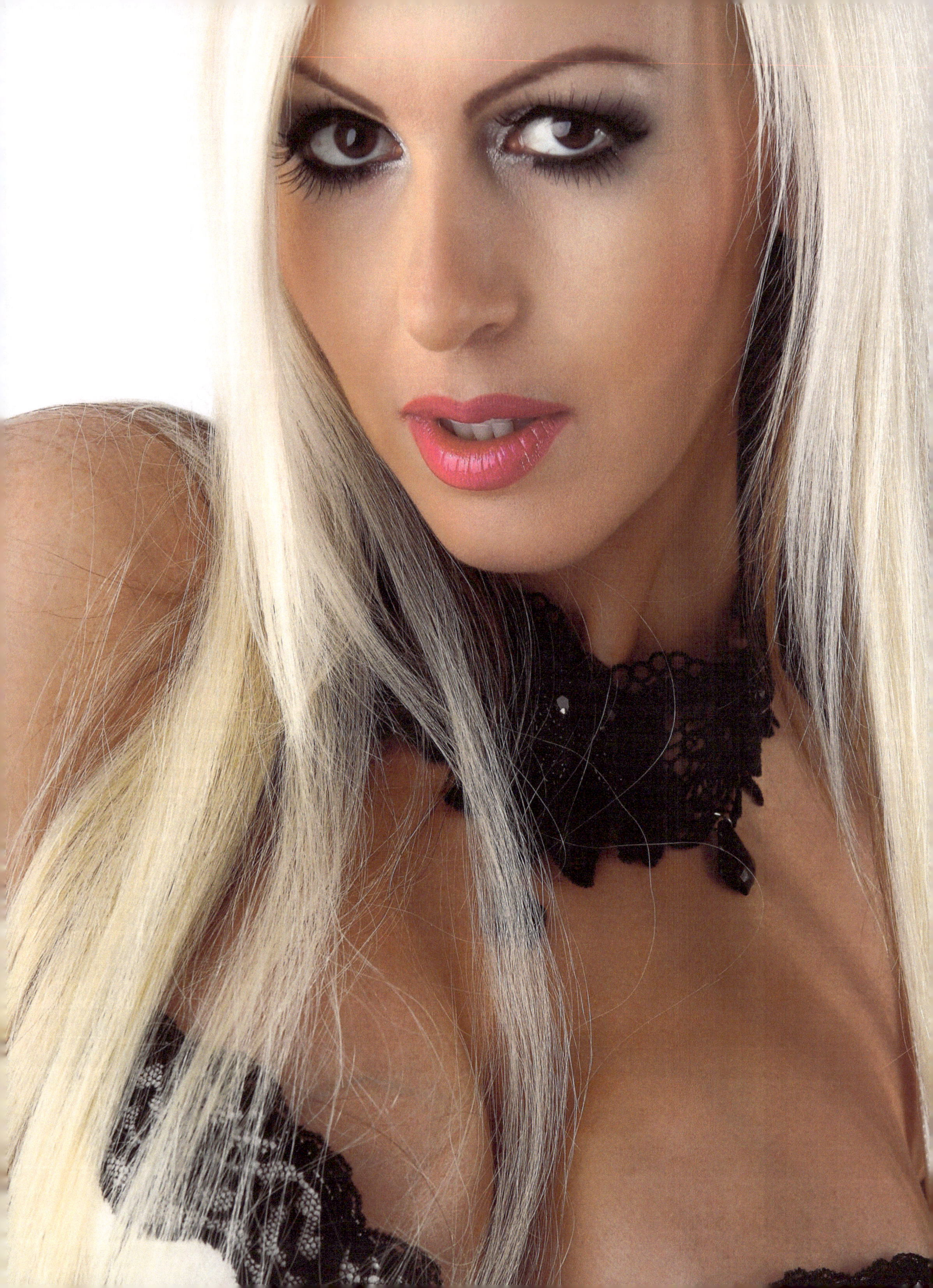

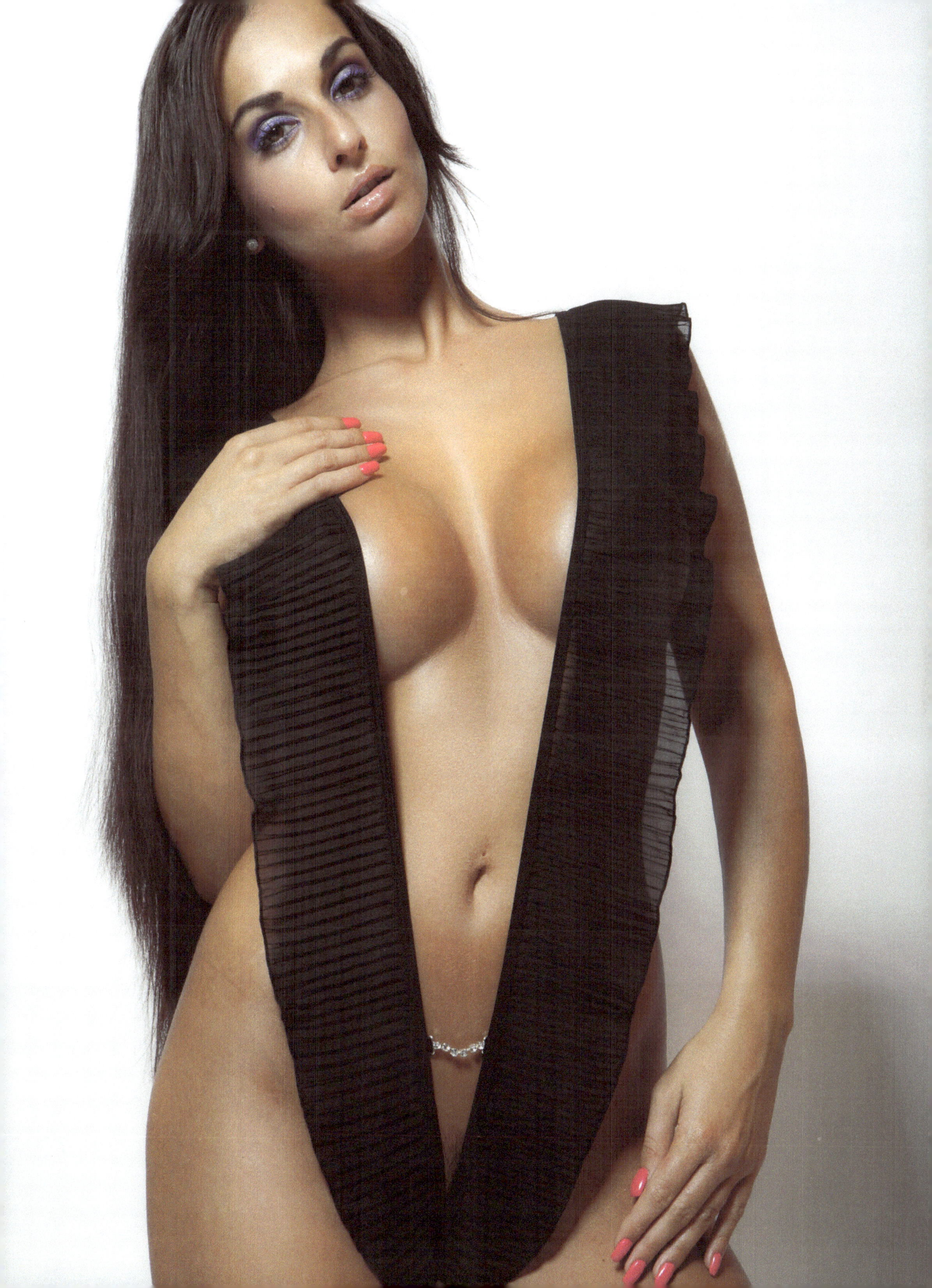

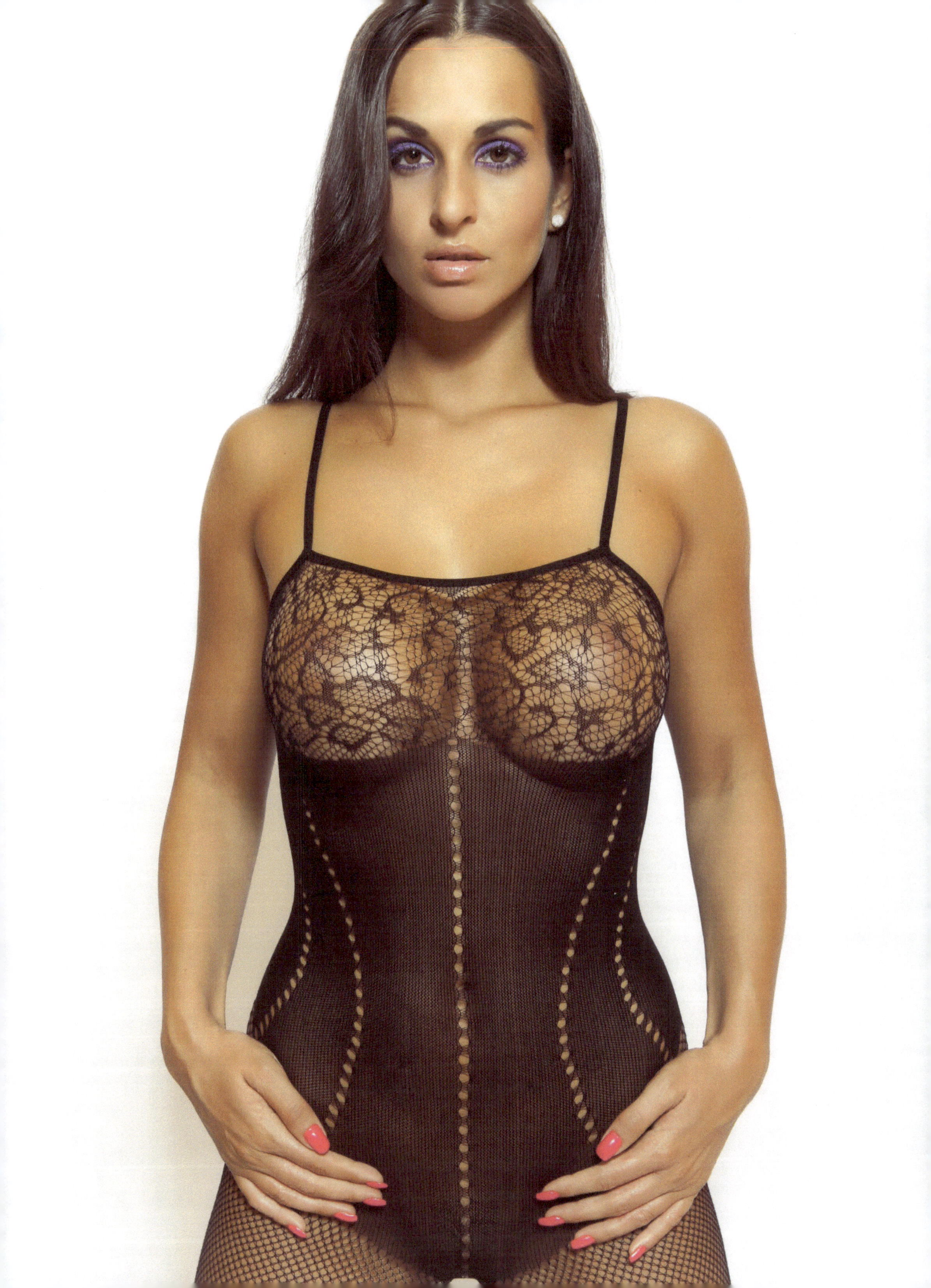

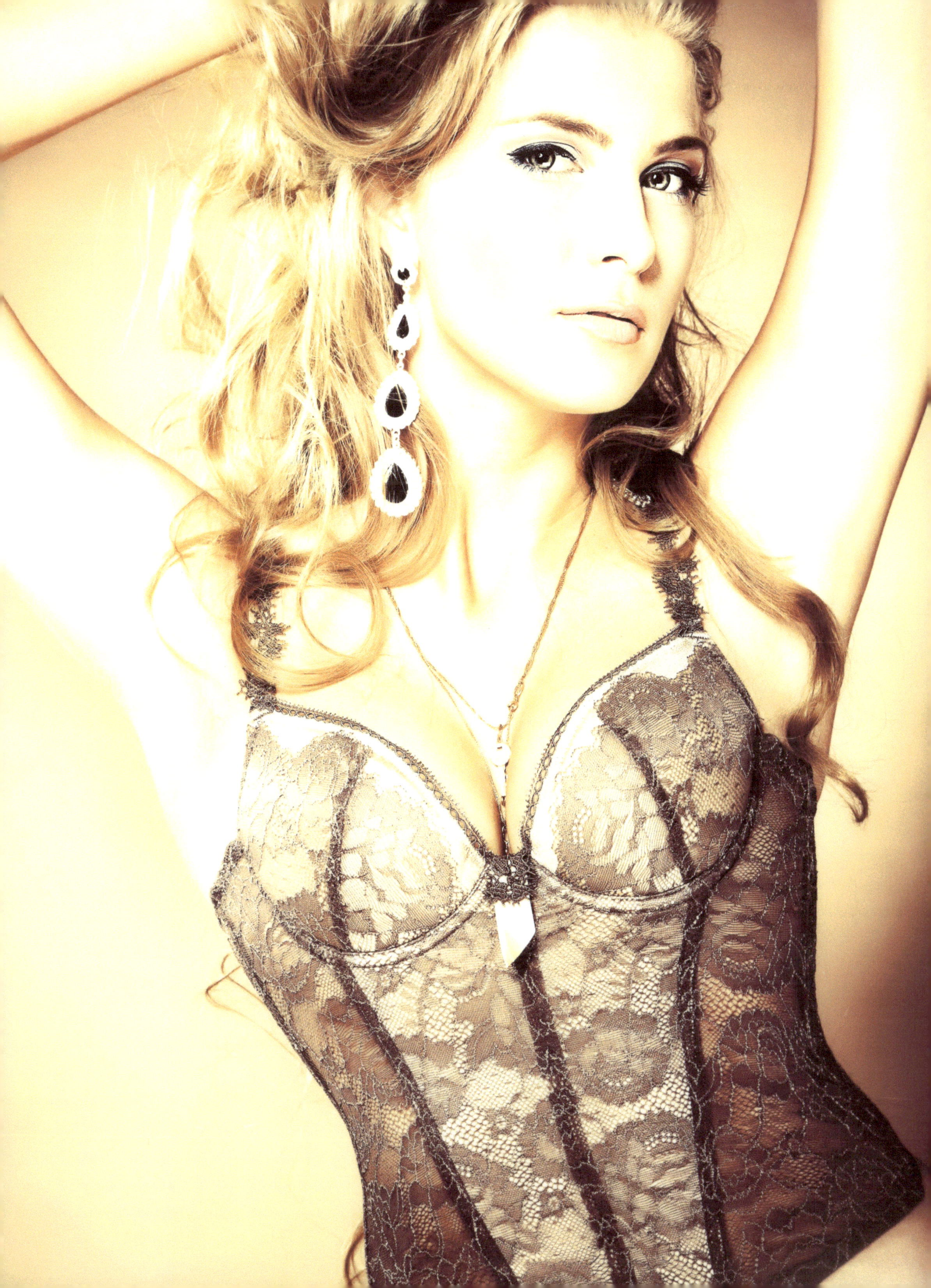

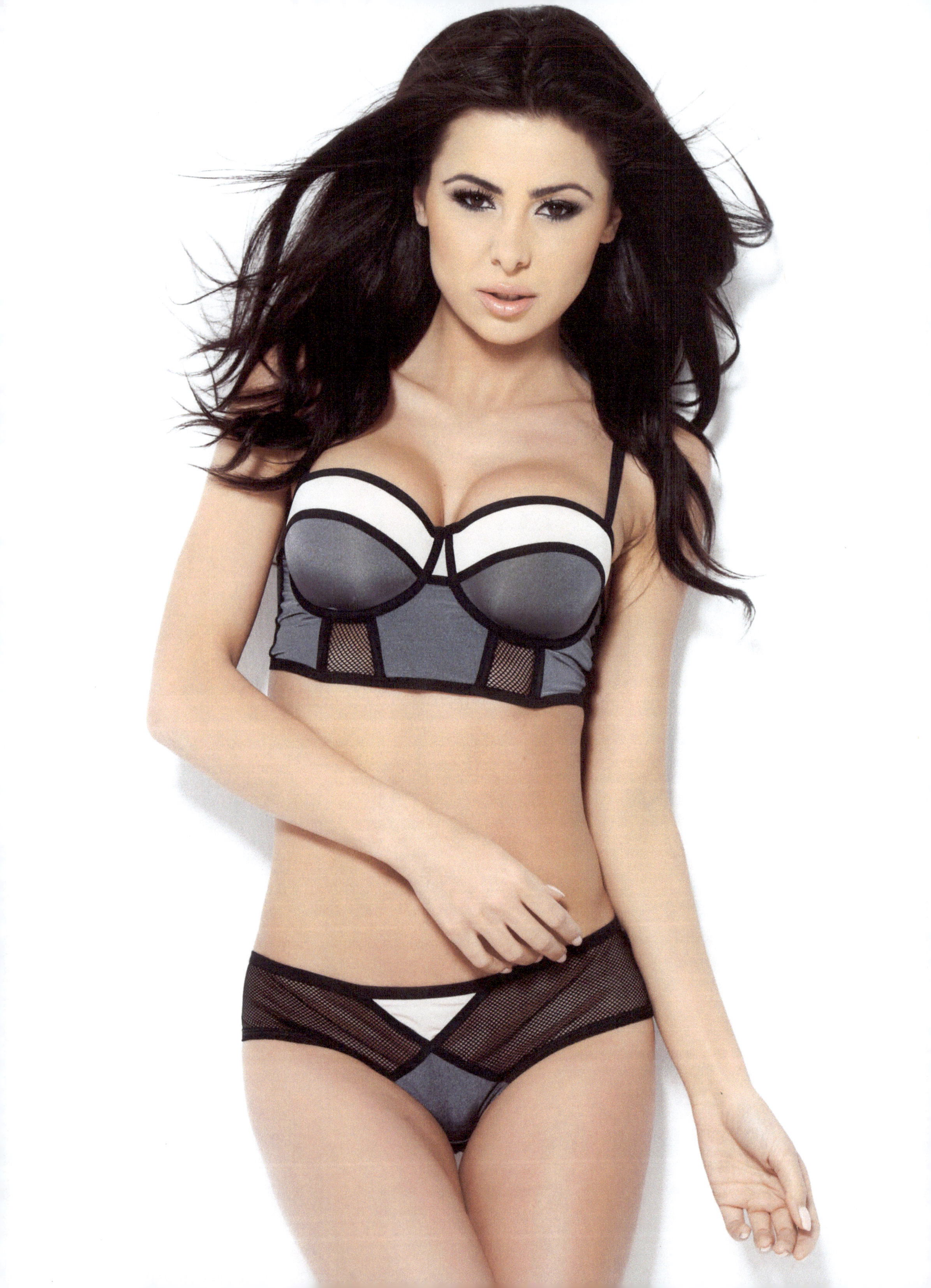

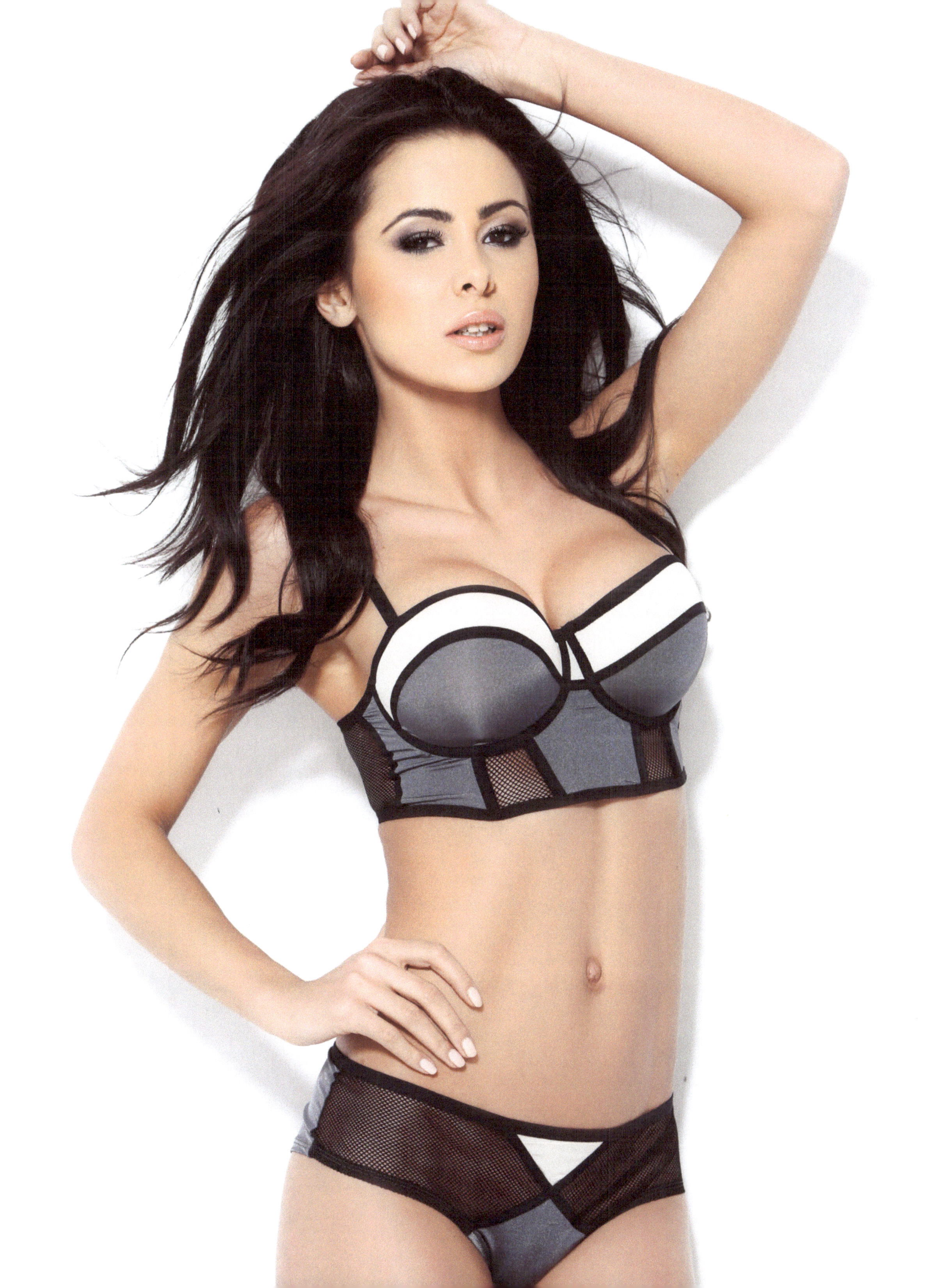

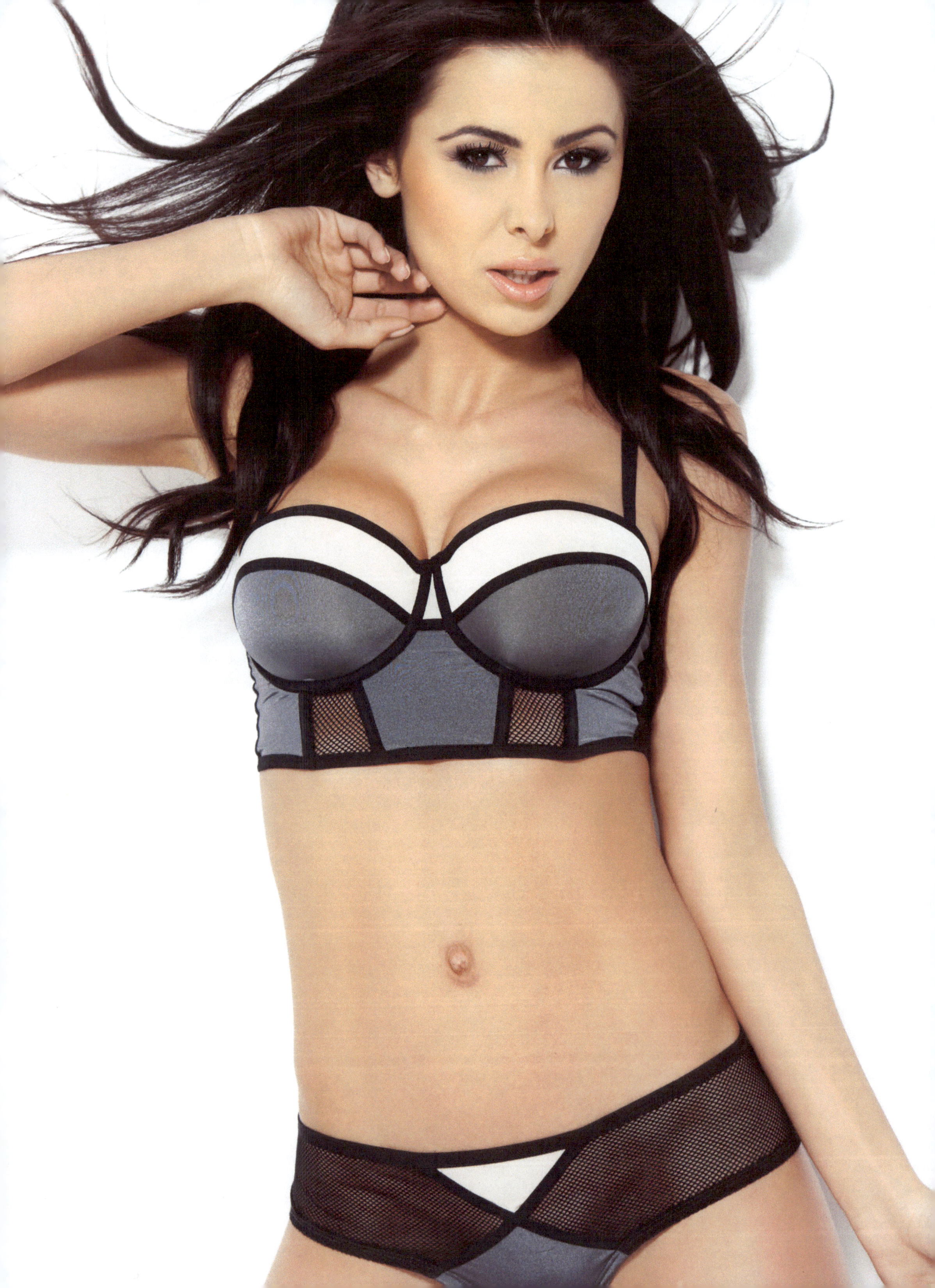

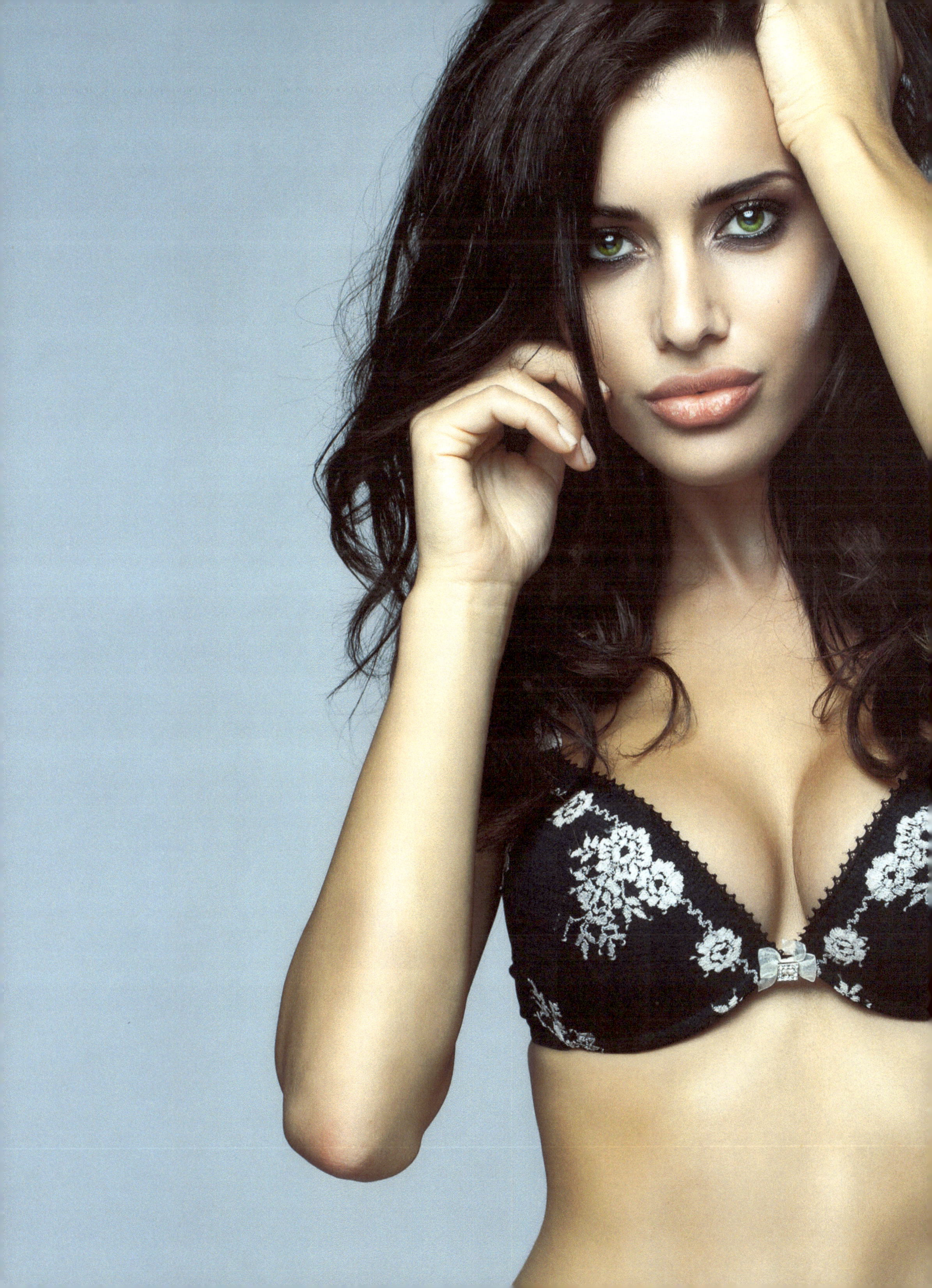

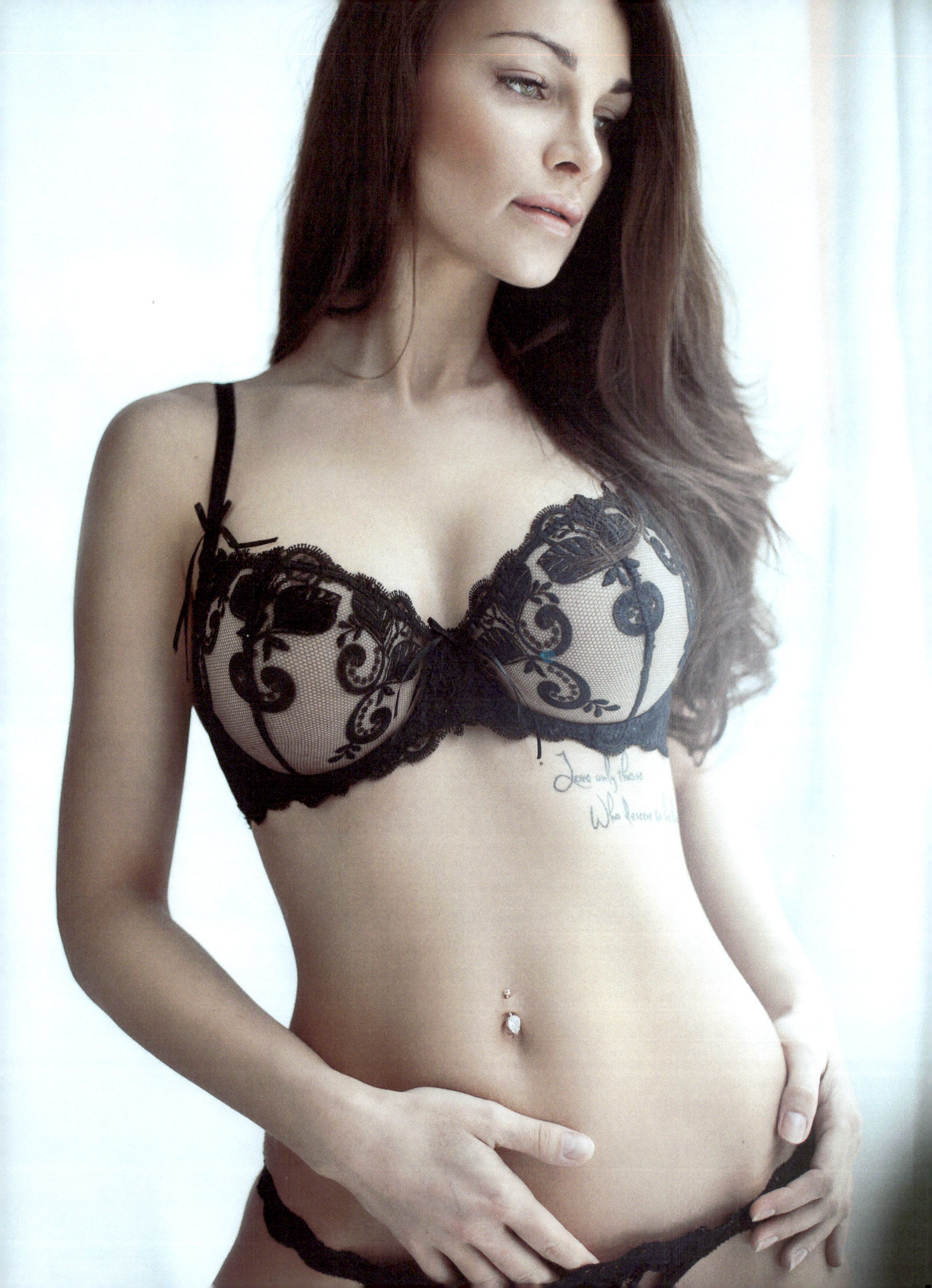
Love only those

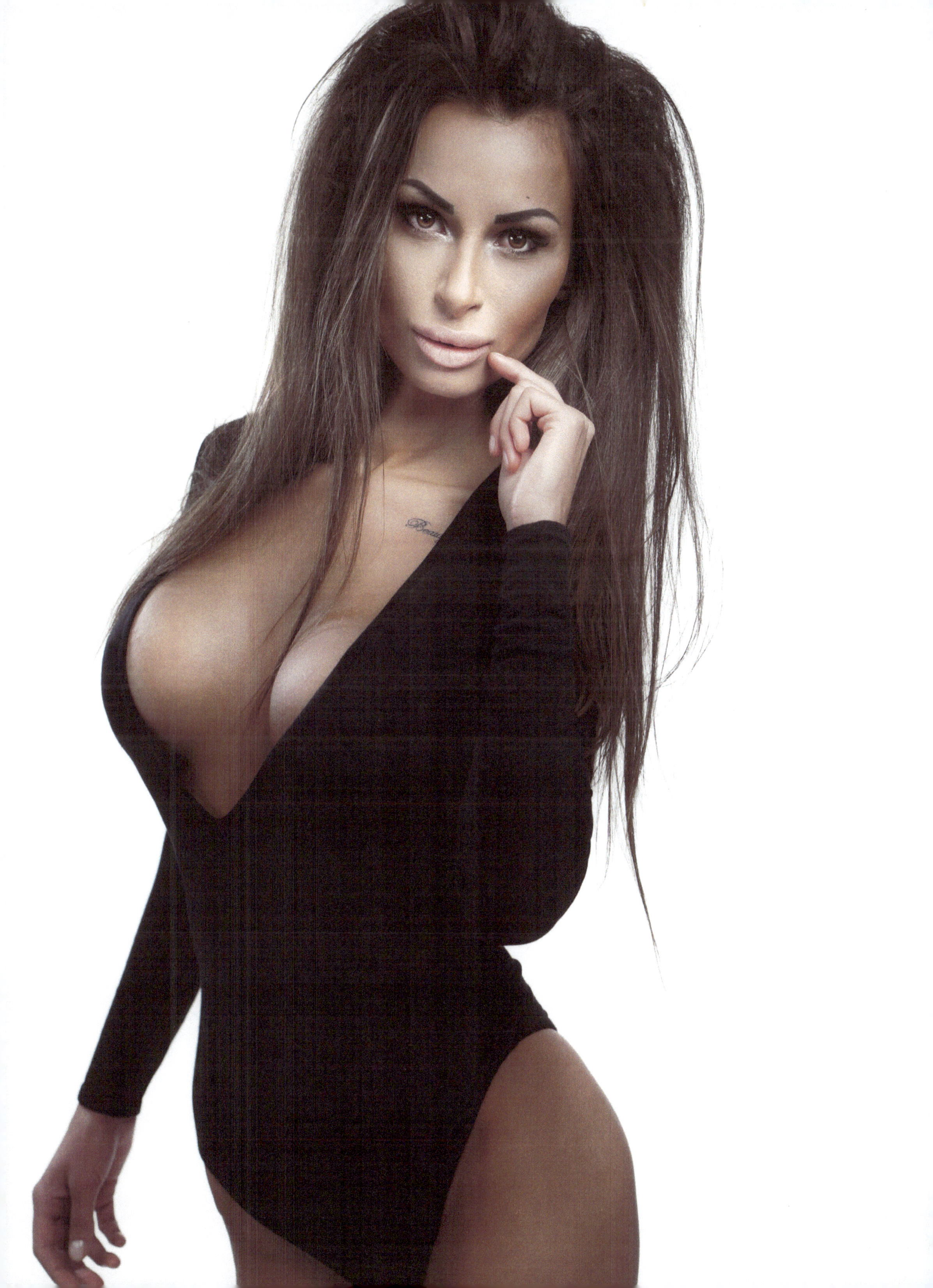

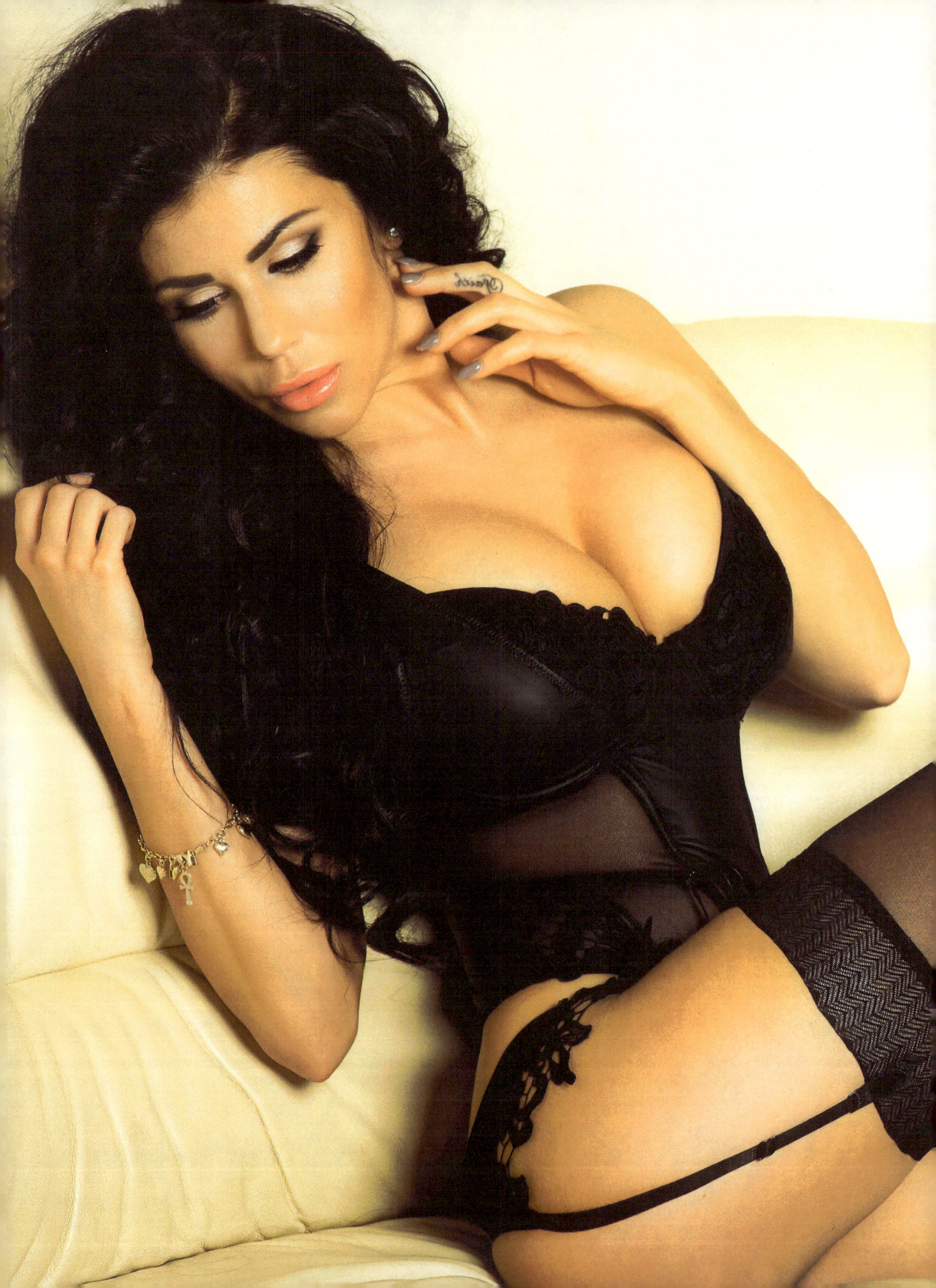

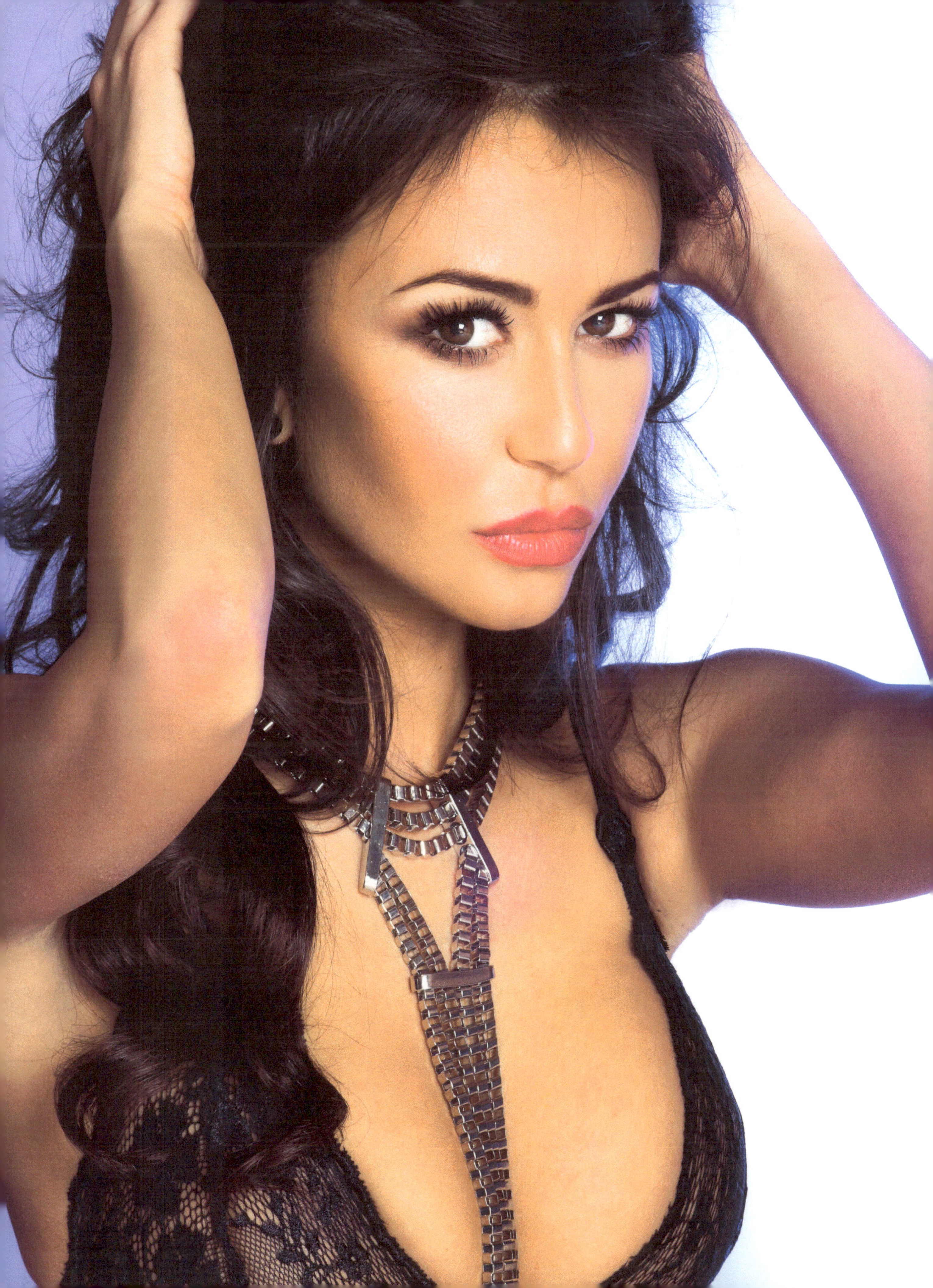

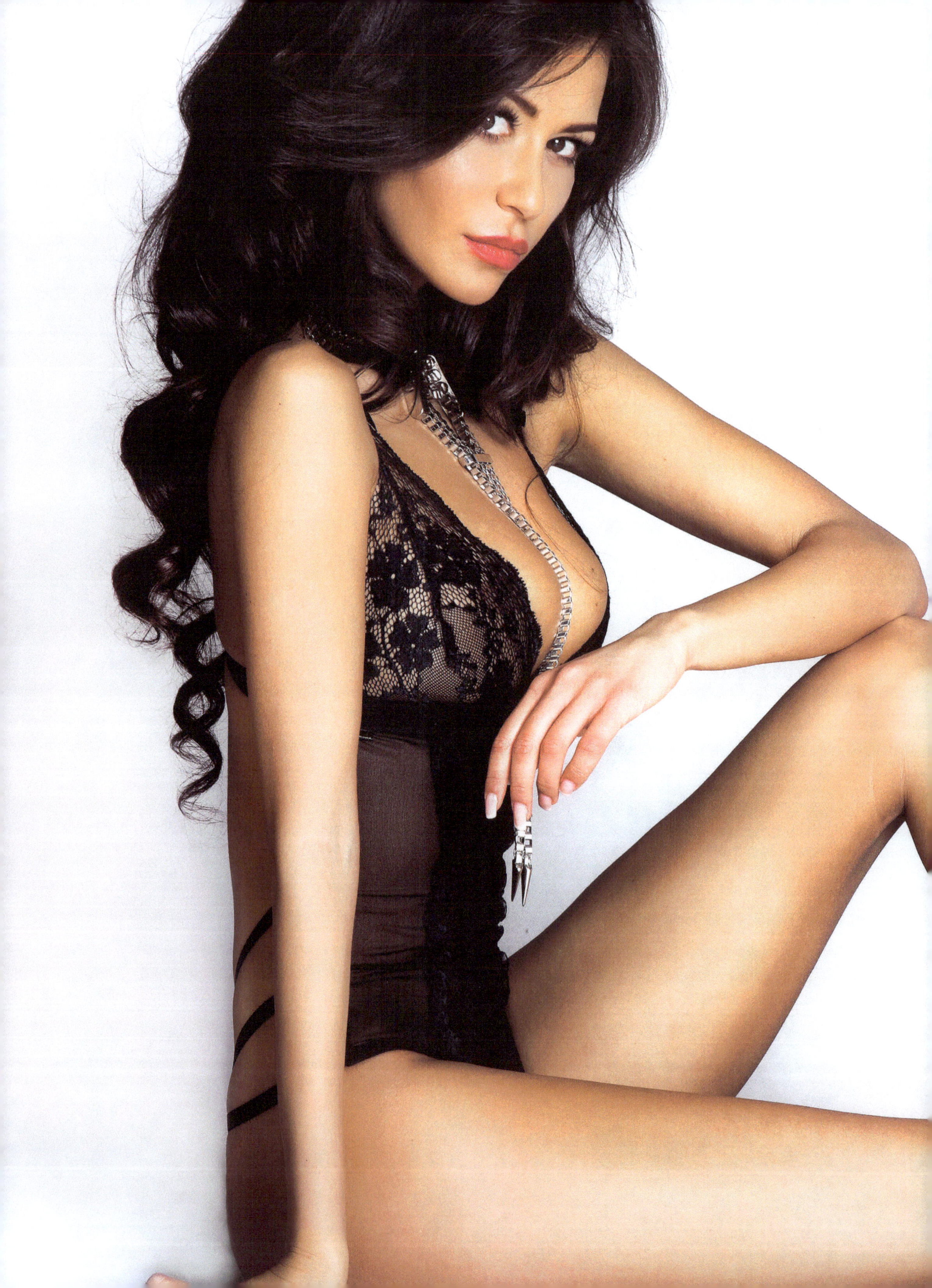

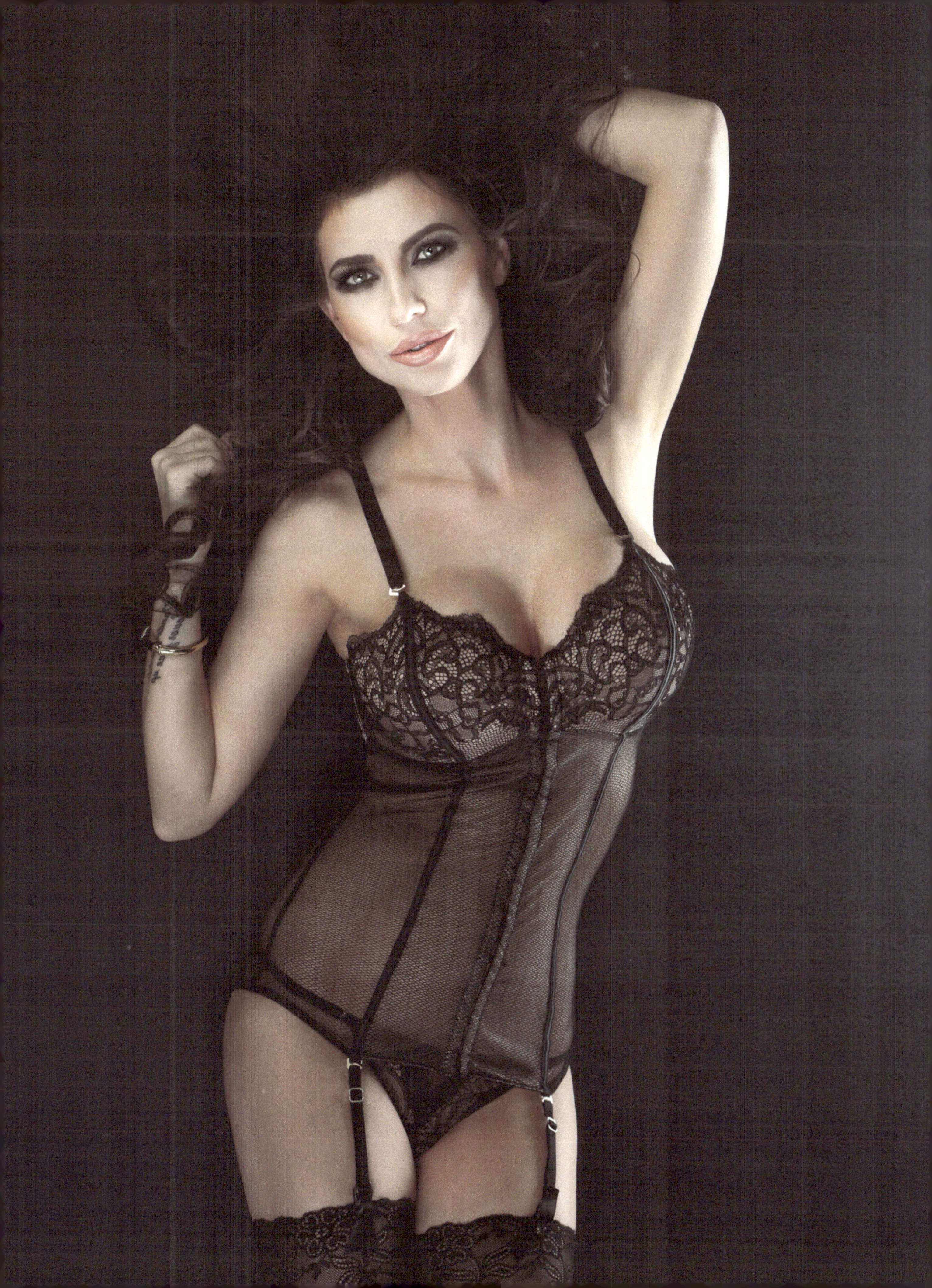

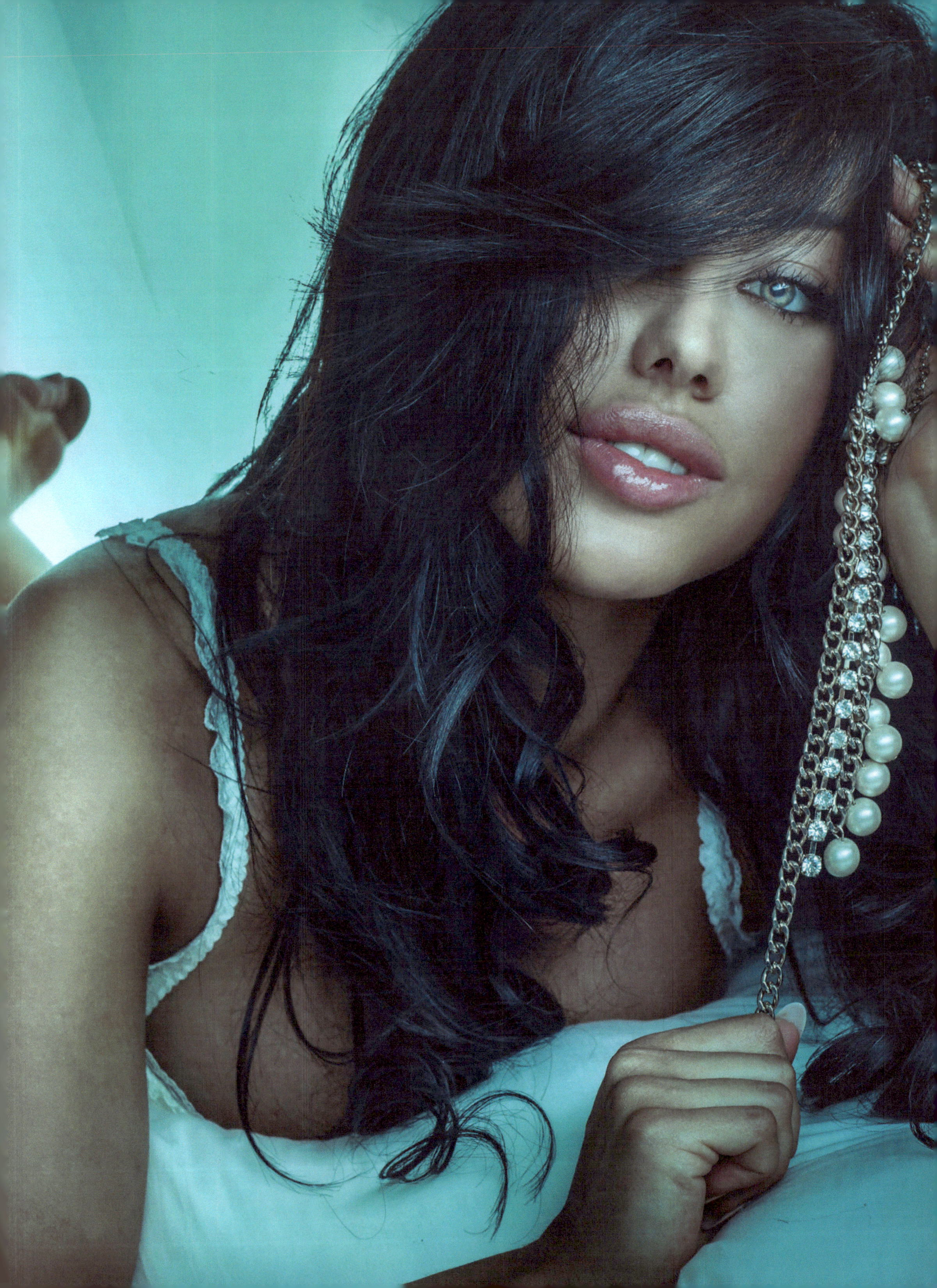

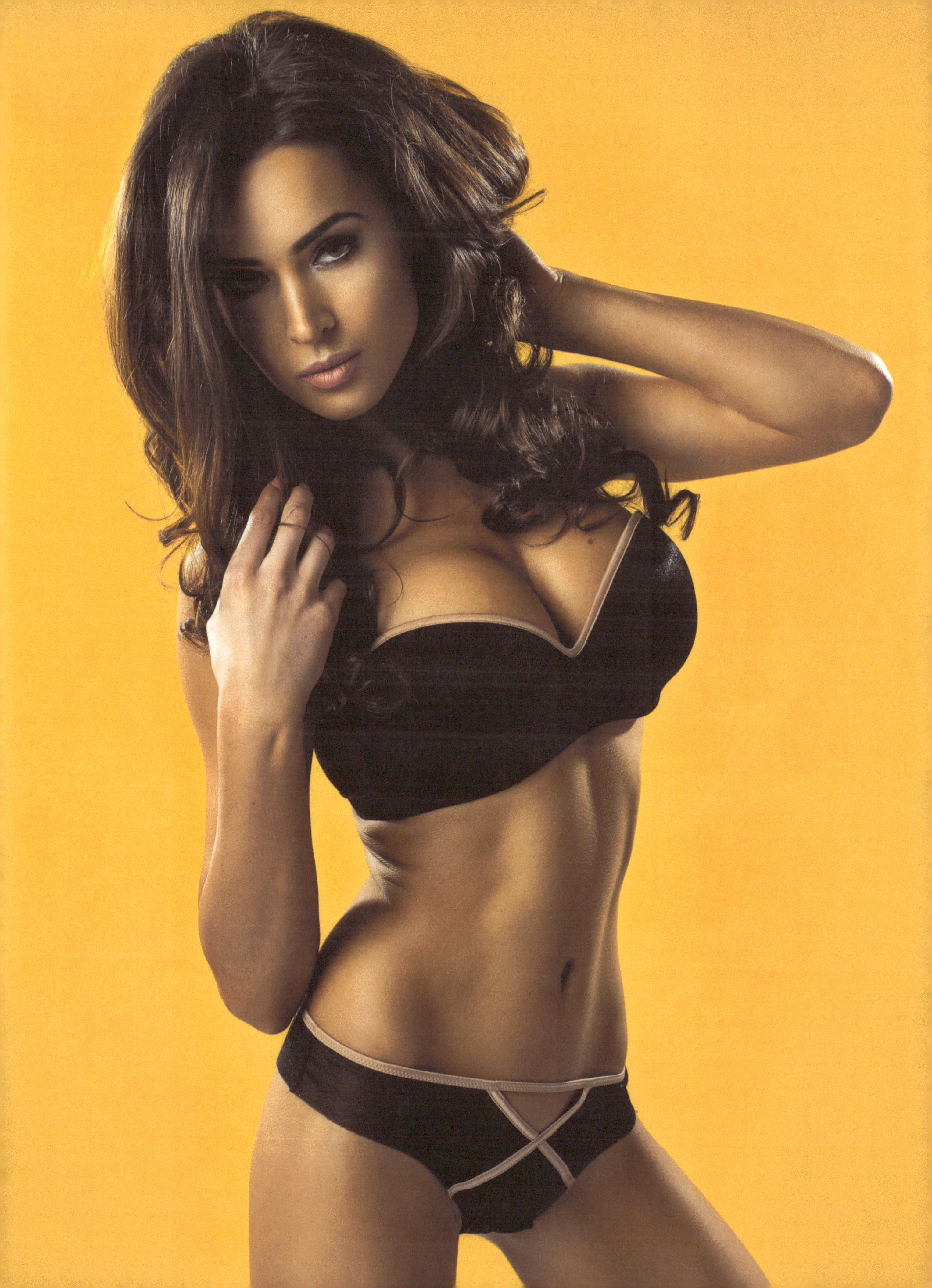

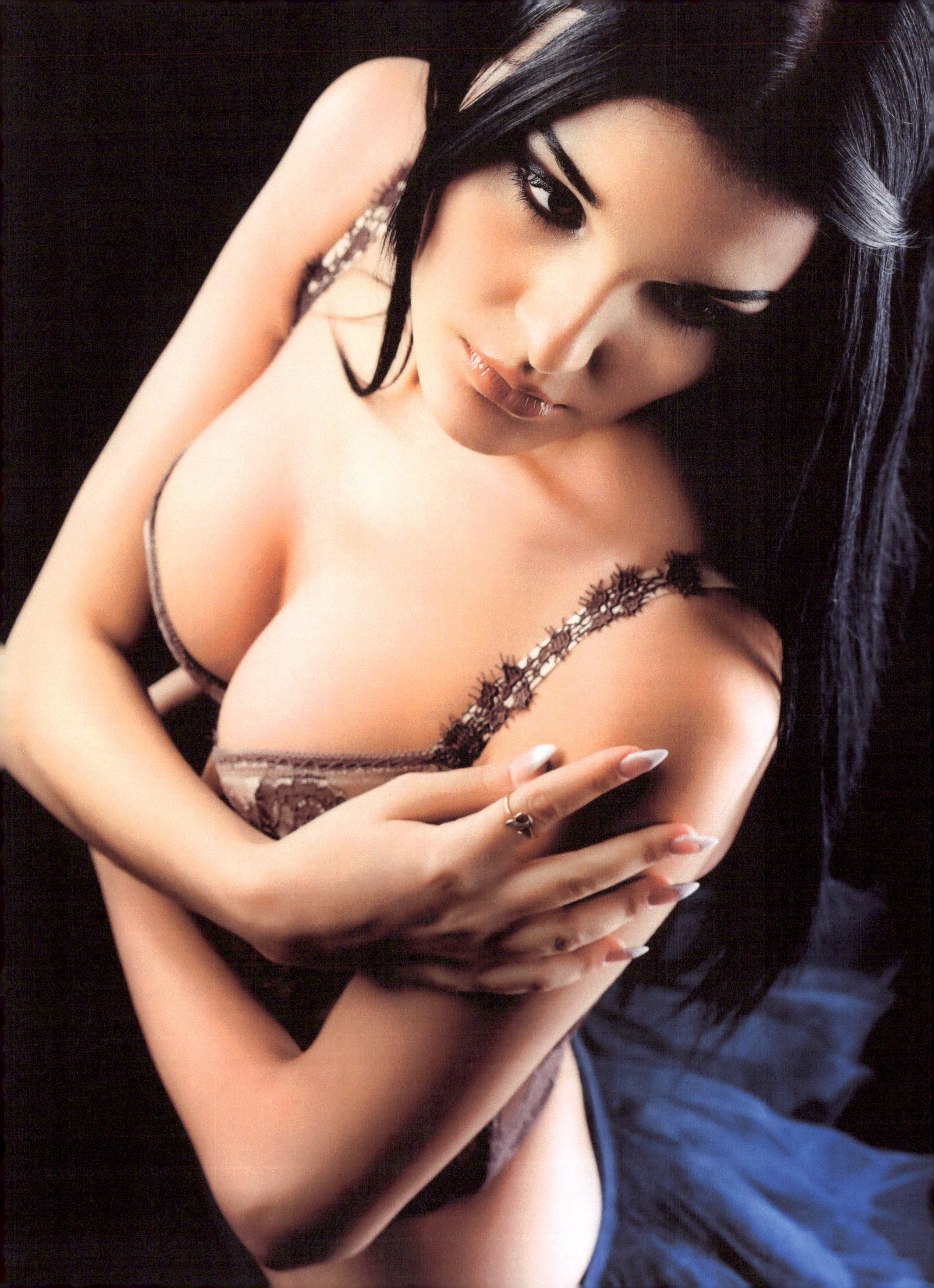

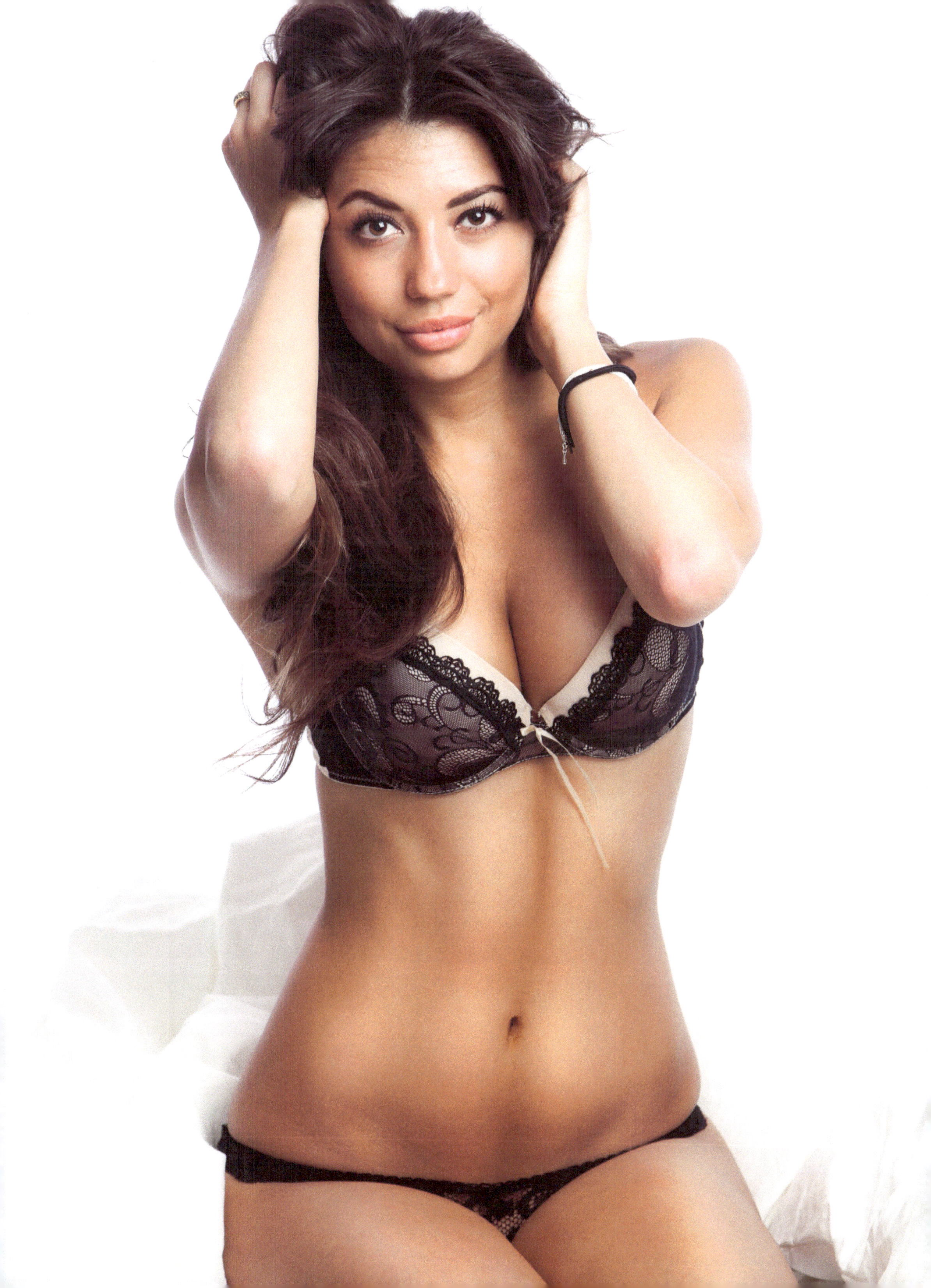

www.ingramcontent.com/pod-product-compliance
Lightning Source LLC
Chambersburg PA
CBHW050418180526
45159CB00005B/2321
* 9 7 8 1 5 3 9 0 8 4 7 5 4 *